EARTH IN DANGER!

Settlements

Polly Goodman

HODDER
Wayland

an imprint of Hodder Children's Books

Titles in the **EARTH IN DANGER!** series

Coasts	Rivers
Energy	Settlements
Farming	Transport

This book is a simplified version of the title *Settlements* in Hodder Wayland's 'Earth Alert' series.

Language level consultant: Norah Granger
Editor: Belinda Hollyer
Designer: Jane Hawkins

Text copyright © 2001 Hodder Wayland
Volume copyright © 2001 Hodder Wayland

First published in 2001 by Hodder Wayland,
an imprint of Hodder Children's Books.

British Library Cataloguing in Publication Data
Goodman, Polly
Settlements. - (Earth in danger!)
1.Human settlements - Juvenile literature 2.Urban ecology - Juvenile literature
I.Title
363.7
ISBN 0 7502 3625 6

Printed in Hong Kong by Wing King Tong

Hodder Children's Books
A division of Hodder Headline Ltd
338 Euston Road, London NW1 3BH

Picture acknowledgements
Cover: main picture Eye Ubiquitous, village Hodder Wayland Picture Library; Alphen aan den Rijn Information 29; Axiom Photographic Agency 17 (Jim Holmes); James Davis Travel Photography 7; Eye Ubiquitous 18 (Paul Hutley), 21 and 24 (Paul Thompson); Getty Images 1 (Jerry Alexander), 4 (Michel Setboun), 5 (Oliver Benn), 10 (Nicholas DeVore), 11 (Sue Cunningham), 16 (Jeremy Walker), 20 (Johan Elzenga), 25 (Robert A Mitchell), 27 (David Hanover); Hodder Wayland Picture Library 3 (Julia Waterlow), 14, 19 Impact Photos 8 (Mark Henley), 9 (Mark Henley), 12 (Alan Keohane),13 (Mark Henley), 15 (Sergio Dorantes), 22 (David Silverberg), 23 (Philip Gordon), 28 (Mark Henley); Alex Robb 6 (both); Stephanie Turner 26 (both). Dustbin information on page 19 courtesy of Ecoschools, Tidy Britain Group. Artwork by Peter Bull Art Studio.

Contents

What are settlements?

Settlements are places where groups of people live. They can be tiny hamlets or villages in the countryside, with only a few houses. Or they can be large towns and cities, with thousands of people.

Settlements in the countryside are called rural settlements. Cities are called urban settlements.

All settlements must be able to get water, food and fuel for cooking. They also need materials to build homes. These are people's basic needs.

These homes in Mongolia belong to people called nomads, who move from place to place. ▼

The history of settlements

People started to live in settlements about 12,000 years ago. Before this they wandered from place to place, hunting animals and gathering plants for food.

Villages and towns grew up near fertile land, where farmers could grow food. Many began beside rivers, which provided water and transport routes. Much later, settlements grew up beside roads and railways.

Some towns grew for special reasons. Ports developed on rivers and coasts where boats came to shore. Industrial towns with factories became manufacturing centres.

▲ The walls of this town in Spain protected its people.

TYPES OF SETTLEMENT

TYPE	NUMBER OF PEOPLE
Hamlet	Fewer than 50
Village	50 to 1,000
Town	1,000 to 100,000
City	Over 100,000

A VILLAGE IN INDONESIA

Kenari is a village on the island of Flores, in Indonesia. Most people are farmers. They grow rice in fields nearby. There is a school, a post office and one small shop in the village.

The houses in Kenari have been built using bamboo and rattan, which are local plants. Since there is no electricity, people cook on fires, burning wood they have gathered nearby. They use oil lamps for light.

There are no roads to Kenari. People have to walk to the nearest market, which is 13 kilometres away.

Houses in Kenari are built on stilts to keep them cool. ▼

Children in Kenari after school. ▶

The growth of cities

Since the 1700s, cities have grown rapidly as centres of manufacturing and business. In the twentieth century, cities grew even faster. Cities have grown because the population of the world has been growing. But they have also grown because more and more people have been moving to cities from the countryside.

Cities attract people because there are more jobs there than in the countryside. There are also many different types of entertainment.

▲ The centre of New York City is an island called Manhattan.

A tiny flat in Tokyo, Japan, the biggest city in the world. ▶

Cities today

Cities are still growing today and they are constantly changing. Every day, workers build new offices and homes. There is so little space that modern buildings are usually tall, so they take up less room on the ground.

In the centre of overcrowded cities, many people live in very small homes. Outside city centres, suburbs are growing and the edges of cities are creeping outwards.

THE TEN MOST CROWDED CITIES IN 2001

Millions of people

1. Tokyo, Japan	29.9
2. Mexico City, Mexico	27.8
3. São Paulo, Brazil	25.3
4. Seoul, South Korea	21.9
5. Mumbai, India	15.3
6. New York, USA	14.6
7. Osaka, Japan	14.2
8. Calcutta, India	14.1
9. Rio de Janeiro, Brazil	14.1
10. Buenos Aires, Argentina	12.9

Activity

HISTORY DETECTIVE

Do you live in a village, town or city? What do you think it was like 100 years ago?
Go to your local library and find the oldest map of where you live. Then compare it with a modern map. What is similar and what is different? Why do you think the settlement grew where it is?

New, tall office blocks and older houses in the city of Shanghai, China. ▼

Cities and the environment

Cities use up huge amounts of energy and produce tonnes of waste every year. Many cities are very polluted. Pollution from traffic and factories that hangs in the air can damage people's health. City waste can pour into rivers and pollute the water, and many cities are running out of places to put their rubbish.

Homes and buildings

Shelter is another basic need. Everyone needs protection from the rain, the sun and the cold.

Thousands of years ago, the first homes were huts made from materials found nearby. Trees were cut down for wood. Clay, earth and stone were dug up from the ground. Many people, especially in poorer countries, still live in homes made just from local materials.

These houses in Lesotho, Africa, are made of stone, earth and wood.▼

SHANTY TOWNS

In poor countries around the world, many people are moving to the cities looking for work. The new arrivals are usually poor and cannot afford to pay for housing. So they build shelters from cheap material they find, including sheets of metal, scraps of wood and plastic.

These settlements are called shanty towns. They are usually on the edges of big cities, built on land that no one else wants.

Modern buildings

Modern buildings include many materials that are made in factories, such as brick, cement, metal, glass and plastic. They are often carried long distances on lorries, trains and ships.

▲ A shanty town on the outskirts of Rio de Janeiro, in Brazil.

As the population increases and people need more homes, we are taking vast quantities of building materials from the environment. Whole forests are cut down, and stone is dug from huge quarries.

Energy

We use energy all the time. We use huge amounts for heating, lighting, cooking, transport, and to run machines.

Energy comes from many different sources. It can come from burning wood, coal, gas or oil. It can also come from the wind, the sun, and moving water.

More energy is used in towns and cities than in smaller settlements. There are more homes, offices, streets and factories, which all need power. Machines such as computers, televisions, fridges and washing machines use up electricity. Cars and lorries burn petrol and oil.

These women in Africa have gathered wood to use for cooking. Wood is their only source of energy. ▼

Running out of energy

Coal, oil and gas are taken from the earth. If we carry on using so much energy, these fuels may run out.

When coal, oil and gas are burnt, they release smoke and gases. This air pollution makes it difficult for some people to breathe. The smoke and gases also rise up into the earth's atmosphere. These 'greenhouse gases' act like a blanket, keeping the earth warm.

As we burn more fuels, many scientists are worried that the earth will get hotter. Polar ice-caps may melt and sea levels may rise, causing floods. If that happens, many parts of the world will become impossible places in which to live.

▲ Cars, buses and lorries cause traffic jams and air pollution in towns and cities.

Food

People in towns and cities rely on farmers in the countryside to grow their food. Wealthy countries can afford to buy food from all around the world so that people have a wide variety to choose from.

Tonnes of food has to be transported into settlements every day using lorries, trains, ships and aeroplanes. Many lorries and ships use refrigerators to keep food cool. All this transport uses up more fuel and causes air pollution (see page 13). Roads become blocked with traffic jams in the cities and the countryside.

◀ Oranges are grown in hot countries and are transported hundreds of thousands of kilometres to supermarkets.

Supermarkets

In wealthy countries, most people now buy their food from large supermarkets. Since there is little space in town and city centres, new supermarkets are usually built on the outskirts. They have car parks so people can drive to them from all over the area.

▲ An 'out of town' shopping centre in Mexico.

Activity

FOOD MAP

Most food from supermarkets has labels telling you the country of origin.

1. Collect food labels from different types of food.
2. Trace a world map from an atlas.
3. Look at the labels, find the countries where each food came from and label them on your map.
4. Draw lines from each country to your own home.

Water

People in towns and cities use huge amounts of water every day. In wealthy countries, water is piped to people's homes from reservoirs or from underground.

WATER USE

This table shows the amount of water used in everyday activities:

Washing hands	0.6 litres
Cleaning teeth	2 litres
Flushing a toilet	9.5 litres
Taking a shower	35 litres
Taking a bath	80 litres
Washing-machine cycle	110 litres
Garden sprinkler	10 litres a minute
Drinking and cooking	10 litres per person per day

Before the water reaches our taps, it passes through treatment works to make it safe to drink. Most used water passes through sewage works before being returned to rivers or the sea.

Sometimes dirty water runs straight into rivers and the sea, polluting the water and killing wildlife. ▶

Not enough water

Rain does not fall equally around the world. People in many countries do not have enough water. Without taps in their homes, many people have to travel long distances to find and carry water.

All water in the world is part of a cycle, called the water cycle. The water we use is replaced by rain. But if we use too much water, it cannot be replaced fast enough. Water levels in rivers and underground are falling because we are using too much water.

▲ Carrying water in Bangladesh.

Activity

1. Add up the amount of water you use every day, using the table on page 16.

2. If you used a bucket that held 9 litres, how many buckets would you need to fill and carry every day if you didn't have taps in your home?

Waste and recycling

People in towns and cities produce tonnes of waste every day, which all has to be taken away.

In many countries, sewage and dirty water pass through sewage works. But sometimes, especially in poorer countries, dirty water runs straight into rivers and the sea, and can cause disease.

Solid waste such as packaging is burned or buried underground. Plastic and other waste stays underground for ever and fills up the ground. Many cities are running out of places to bury their rubbish. Rubbish dumps can pollute the air and water, and cause disease.

A bulldozer burying rubbish in a dump, called a landfill site. ▶

Recycling

Recycling changes some types of rubbish into material that can be used again. It can help reduce the waste that we bury underground.

Paper, glass, plastic, aluminium and tin cans can all be recycled. To recycle, we have to separate the material that can be recycled from the rest of our rubbish.

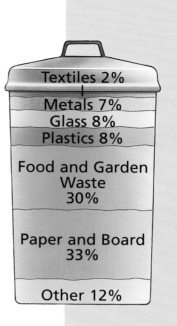

Textiles 2%
Metals 7%
Glass 8%
Plastics 8%
Food and Garden Waste 30%
Paper and Board 33%
Other 12%

A TYPICAL DUSTBIN

This is the content of an average dustbin from a house in a wealthy country.

▲Rubbish is separated into a recycling lorry.

TRUE STORY

FORT LAUDERDALE, FLORIDA

Fort Lauderdale is a city in Florida, USA, which has a recycling scheme. Every home is given a special bin for people to put rubbish that can be recycled. Every week, the bins are collected and emptied, free of charge.

The city also has a group called the 'Recycle Corps', who encourage people to recycle as much as possible. There is information about recycling and a special logo.

City zones

Large cities often have different areas, or zones, each with a special function. Most people work in a commercial zone, where there are shops, banks and offices. Areas of factories and workshops are called industrial zones.

Areas where most of the buildings are homes are called residential. The oldest residential areas are close to the city centre, called the inner city.

The chimneys of an industrial zone behind a residential area.▼

Travelling across the city

Thousands of people travel to work in cities every day. Many travel from one side of a city to another. Others travel in from the countryside, or towns outside the city.

Cars, buses, trains and bicycles carry people to work. Roads often become blocked by traffic jams, especially in the rush hours, and the air can be filled with unpleasant traffic fumes.

People who use public transport, such as trains and buses, help reduce the amount of air pollution and congestion in cities. They reduce the number of vehicles needed to carry people around.

▲ Office workers in the morning rush hour in London.

Entertainment and leisure

Every city has many different ways for people to spend their spare time. Indoors there are cinemas, theatres, bars and restaurants.

Outside areas include parks, playgrounds, sports fields and swimming pools. Parks are also habitats for plants and animals.

Central Park, in the middle of New York City.▼

▲An aerial
view across
Tokyo, the
world's most
populated city.

Planning growth

Many cities around the world are growing too fast.
But others are controlled by planners, who usually
work for the government. Planners decide whether new
buildings should be built, and where they will be.

There are different ideas about planning cities. Some
people think residential areas should be kept separate
from commercial zones, to make residential areas more
attractive places to live. Others believe people should
live close to their work, so they travel less and there is
less traffic.

Changing cities

Cities all over the world are getting bigger, because populations grow and more people move to cities from the countryside. Today, about 50 per cent of the world's population live in cities. By 2010 this figure is expected to grow to 55 per cent.

▲ High-rise blocks of flats in Hong Kong.

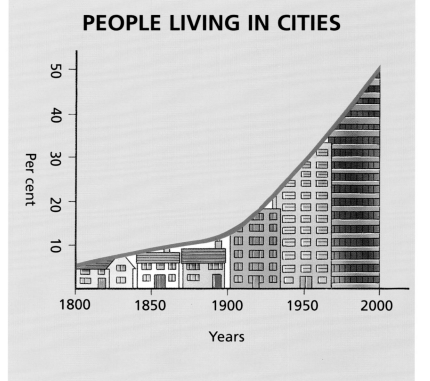

PEOPLE LIVING IN CITIES

Per cent

50 40 30 20 10

1800 1850 1900 1950 2000

Years

In city centres, where there is very little space, new buildings are often high-rise blocks. They can fit more homes for people on a small area of land than lower buildings provide.

Out of town

Since the early 1980s, many businesses have moved out of crowded city centres to business parks on the city outskirts. Business parks have space for car parks, so most people drive there to work.

Out-of-town business parks reduce congestion in city centres, but they increase the amount of traffic on roads because more people use cars to get to work. This causes congestion and pollution (see page 13).

A business park on the edge of a city.▼

Inner-city redevelopment

In many inner-city areas, where businesses have moved out, jobs have disappeared and areas have become poorer. Some are now being improved. Old buildings are being pulled down or improved, and new ones built. Inner cities are becoming more attractive places in which to live and work.

A CITY WILDLIFE PARK

Camley Street Natural Park is in the centre of London, Britain's capital city. It is a nature reserve, with a pond, meadows and woods. These provide a habitat for wild plants and animals, such as frogs, butterflies and bees.

The park was once used to store coal. Then it was a rubbish tip. Now it is a protected area where children can study wildlife in the middle of a city.

▲ Camley Street Natural Park is near Kings Cross railway station in London.

A photographer takes a photo of wildlife in the park. ▶

Working in different places

Advances in technology mean that many people do not have to work in city centres any more. Email and the Internet allow people to work anywhere they like and use computers to keep in touch with offices.

Many people are starting to work from home. Businesses are moving out of city centres to the countryside or smaller towns. Computers are reducing the amount of travelling people do, so they are helping to reduce traffic congestion and pollution.

▲ This man is working from home using a laptop computer.

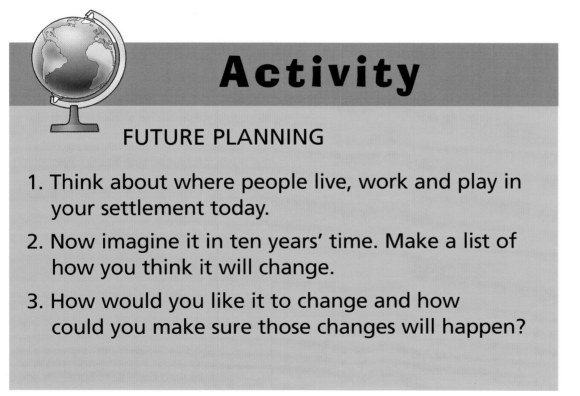

Activity

FUTURE PLANNING

1. Think about where people live, work and play in your settlement today.

2. Now imagine it in ten years' time. Make a list of how you think it will change.

3. How would you like it to change and how could you make sure those changes will happen?

The future

Since towns and cities are constantly growing, we have to keep looking for better ways to protect our environment. If not, we will exhaust the earth's natural resources of food, energy and water, and pollute the environment with traffic fumes and waste.

We should be careful about how much energy and water we use every day. We should try to produce less waste and recycle more rubbish. Our cities need to be carefully planned, and new buildings need to be controlled. If this happens, our cities will be attractive places in which to live and work.

▲
An overcrowded street in Tokyo, Japan.

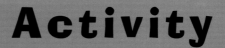

Activity

You can find out how your city, town or village is protecting the environment and planning for the future. Start by asking your local council about it. You could ask questions like these:

● Is there a waste recycling scheme?

● Are any areas going to be improved for the future?

● What new developments are planned?

AN ENVIRONMENTALLY FRIENDLY TOWN

Ecolonia is a small town in the Netherlands, which was built between 1991 and 1992. It was built to show how a settlement could work with little damage to the environment.

People are allowed to drive cars to their homes, but not through the town centre. So most of the streets are just for walkers and cyclists.

The residents recycle almost all their rubbish, and most of the houses have solar panels to heat their water.

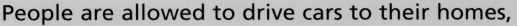

▲ Houses around the lake in Ecolonia.

Other towns in the Netherlands are copying ideas from Ecolonia to make them more environmentally friendly.

Glossary

Basic needs The things all people need to survive.

Congestion Too many vehicles or people in a small space.

Country of origin The country where something was grown or made.

Environment Everything in our surroundings.

Environmentally friendly Not damaging to the environment.

Fumes Gas or smoke that is harmful or smells unpleasant.

Greenhouse gases Gases which trap the sun's warmth near the surface of the earth.

Habitat The natural home of a plant or animal.

Industrial A process involved with making goods, usually in factories.

Landfill site Rubbish dump where solid waste is buried underground.

Nomads People who do not live permanently in one place.

Pollution Damage to air, water and land by harmful materials.

Recycle To return used materials to be remade and used again.

Rural Belonging to the countryside.

Rush hour Busy times in the mornings and evenings when people travel to and from work.

Solar panels Solar panels use energy from the sun's rays to produce electricity. It does not create pollution.

Suburbs Communities next to, or near, a city.

Waste All the material we need to get rid of, like packaging.

30

Further information

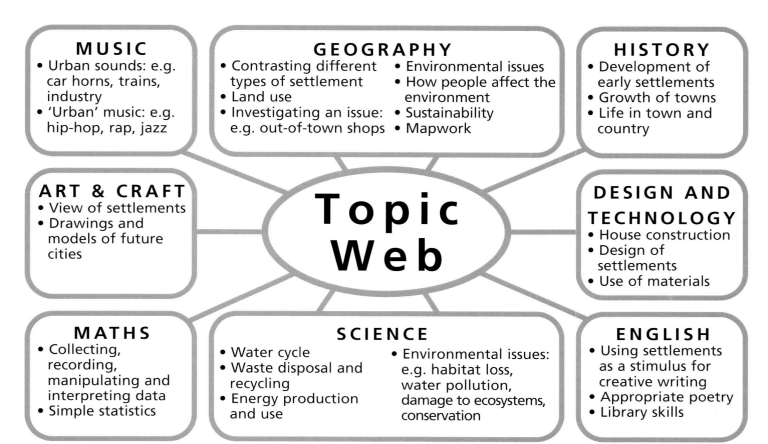

MUSIC
- Urban sounds: e.g. car horns, trains, industry
- 'Urban' music: e.g. hip-hop, rap, jazz

GEOGRAPHY
- Contrasting different types of settlement
- Land use
- Investigating an issue: e.g. out-of-town shops
- Environmental issues
- How people affect the environment
- Sustainability
- Mapwork

HISTORY
- Development of early settlements
- Growth of towns
- Life in town and country

ART & CRAFT
- View of settlements
- Drawings and models of future cities

Topic Web

DESIGN AND TECHNOLOGY
- House construction
- Design of settlements
- Use of materials

MATHS
- Collecting, recording, manipulating and interpreting data
- Simple statistics

SCIENCE
- Water cycle
- Waste disposal and recycling
- Energy production and use
- Environmental issues: e.g. habitat loss, water pollution, damage to ecosystems, conservation

ENGLISH
- Using settlements as a stimulus for creative writing
- Appropriate poetry
- Library skills

Other books to read

Building Amazing Structures series: Bridge, Canal, Dam, Tunnel, Skyscraper, Stadium by Chris Oxlade (Heinemann, 2000)

Earth Care: People and Society (Heinemann, 1999)

Local Studies in History and Geography series: People and Communities, People and Buildings by R. Rees and J. Withersby (Heinemann, 1996)

Saving our World: New Energy Sources by N. Hawkes (Watts, 2000)

Themes in Geography: Settlements by Fred Martin (Heinemann, 1996)

World Cities series: Beijing, Berlin, London, Moscow, New York, Paris, Rome, Sydney by Christine Hatt (Belitha, 1999)

The World's Top Ten Cites by Neil Morris (Belitha 1999)

Zoom City by Rob Alcraft (Heinemann 1998)

Index